Mapping of Erosion Features Related to Thaw of Permafrost in the Noatak National Preserve, Alaska

Natural Resource Data Series NPS/ARCN/NRDS—2012/248

David K. Swanson

National Park Service
Fairbanks Administrative Center
4175 Geist Road
Fairbanks, Alaska 99709

February, 2012

U.S. Department of the Interior
National Park Service
Natural Resource Stewardship and Science
Fort Collins, Colorado

The National Park Service, Natural Resource Stewardship and Science office in Fort Collins, Colorado, publishes a range of reports that address natural resource topics of interest and applicability to a broad audience in the National Park Service and others in natural resource management, including scientists, conservation and environmental constituencies, and the public.

The Natural Resource Data Series is intended for the timely release of basic data sets and data summaries. Care has been taken to assure accuracy of raw data values, but a thorough analysis and interpretation of the data has not been completed. Consequently, the initial analyses of data in this report are provisional and subject to change.

All manuscripts in the series receive the appropriate level of peer review to ensure that the information is scientifically credible, technically accurate, appropriately written for the intended audience, and designed and published in a professional manner.

This report received informal peer review by subject-matter experts who were not directly involved in the collection, analysis, or reporting of the data.

Views, statements, findings, conclusions, recommendations, and data in this report do not necessarily reflect views and policies of the National Park Service, U.S. Department of the Interior. Mention of trade names or commercial products does not constitute endorsement or recommendation for use by the U.S. Government.

This report is available from the National Park Service, Arctic Inventory and Monitoring Network (http://science.nature.nps.gov/im/units/arcn/) and the Natural Resource Publications Management website (http://www.nature.nps.gov/publications/nrpm/).

Please cite this publication as:

Swanson, D. K. 2012. Mapping of erosion features related to thaw of permafrost in the Noatak National Preserve, Alaska. Natural Resource Data Series NPS/ARCN/NRDS—2012/248. National Park Service, Fort Collins, Colorado.

NPS 189/112839,February2012

Contents

Figures

Abstract

A systematic survey was made of the Noatak National Preserve (NOAT) in northern Alaska for active-layer detachments (ALD) and retrogressive thaw slumps (RTS) using high-resolution satellite imagery from 2006 through 2008. ALD and RTS develop by localized thaw of permafrost, and have the potential to expose significant areas of soil to erosion. I identified 848 active-layer detachments in the Preserve, exposing a total area of 103 ha of bare soil. ALD were most common on well vegetated, moderate slopes (average slope 16%) with southwest aspect. They occur predominantly in ecological subsections (Jorgenson *et al.* 2001) consisting of hills or mountains composed of clastic sedimentary rocks. A total of 276 retrogressive thaw slumps were identified, exposing an area of 90 ha of bare soil. The RTS occur in thick Pleistocene sediments (mainly glacial till and glacial lake deposits), primarily along rivers and lakes, though some occur in uplands away from water. RTS were also mapped on 1977 color-infrared aerial photography for a 190-square-kilometer study area in NOAT. RTS in this area increased from 23 slumps covering 13.5 ha in 1977 to 35 slumps covering 21.2 ha in 2006-2008.

Introduction

Thaw of permafrost can lead to subsidence, mass movement of material on slopes, and exposure of bare soil to erosion by water. While localized thaw and refreezing of permafrost occurs under a stable cold arctic climate, climate change has been cited as a cause of recent increased thaw of permafrost in Alaska (Jorgenson et al., 2006). Concerns about the state of permafrost in the future led the National Park Service Arctic Inventory and Monitoring Network (ARCN, Fig. 1), to include permafrost as a monitoring "Vital Sign" (Lawler et al., 2009). Thaw-related slumping and associated soil erosion may have increased in ARCN in recent years (Balser et al., 2007), and an important component of ARCN's permafrost vital sign monitoring involves locating and mapping subsidence and erosion features related to permafrost thaw.

Two important erosion features related to permafrost thaw in NOAT are active-layer detachments (ALD) and retrogressive thaw slumps (RTS)(Balser et al., 2010; Swanson and Hill, 2010; Swanson, 2012). ALD are small landslides that occur on vegetated slopes (Fig. 2). A surface layer roughly 1 m thick slides as a unit held together by the root mat, and accumulates as a winkled mass on the footslope. ALD are typically 10 to 30 meters wide and from tens to several hundred meters long. The slide leaves an elongated region of bare soil exposed on a slope, which can lead to erosion of sediment into streams (Bowden et al., 2008; Lamoureux and Lafrenière, 2009). ALD tend to occur in clusters, where soil and slope conditions are favorable, after periods of unusually warm summer weather or possibly high rainfall (Carter and Galloway, 1981; Lewkowicz and Harris, 2005). They probably occur after thaw of the ice-rich layer that is often present in the upper permafrost (approximately 1 m below the surface), which produces a mud slurry that lubricates the downslope flow of an elongate strip of cohesive surface soil and vegetation (Lewkowicz and Harris, 2005; Lewkowicz, 2007).

Retrogressive thaw slumps occur where a cut-bank in ice-rich permafrost advances into undisturbed ground as material thaws in the steep bank, falls or slumps onto the adjacent more gentle slope, and then is transported away by water erosion or sliding (Burn and Lewkowicz, 1990; Fig. 3). RTS are deeper than ALD, and the eroding cut-bank is typically 2 to 10 m high. RTS often begin as an escarpment produced by marine, lakeshore, or riverbank erosion, or by an ALD. As they advance by thawing and slumping, they can shed large amounts of sediment into the adjacent water body and also affect water chemistry (Crosby, 2009; Kokelj et al., 2005). The warming effect of a water body on the permafrost may also make shorelines favorable to the development of RTS (Kokelj et al., 2009). Very ice-rich material of substantial thickness (e.g., several meters) and lateral extent is needed to produce a RTS.

The newly acquired, nearly complete coverage of ARCN by high-resolution satellite imagery has allowed the NPS to make a comprehensive survey of erosion features caused by permafrost thaw in the Noatak National Preserve (NOAT). I combined automated mapping methods with visual recognition of geomorphic features to make a comprehensive map of ALD and RTS in NOAT. The purpose of this report is to present the results of mapping in NOAT. Mapping in three other NPS units (Bering Land Bridge National Preserve (BELA), Cape Krusenstern National Monument (CAKR), and Kobuk Valley National Park (KOVA) was reported previously (Swanson, 2010). Mapping continues in the remaining ARCN NPS unit, Gates of the Arctic National Park and Preserve (GAAR).

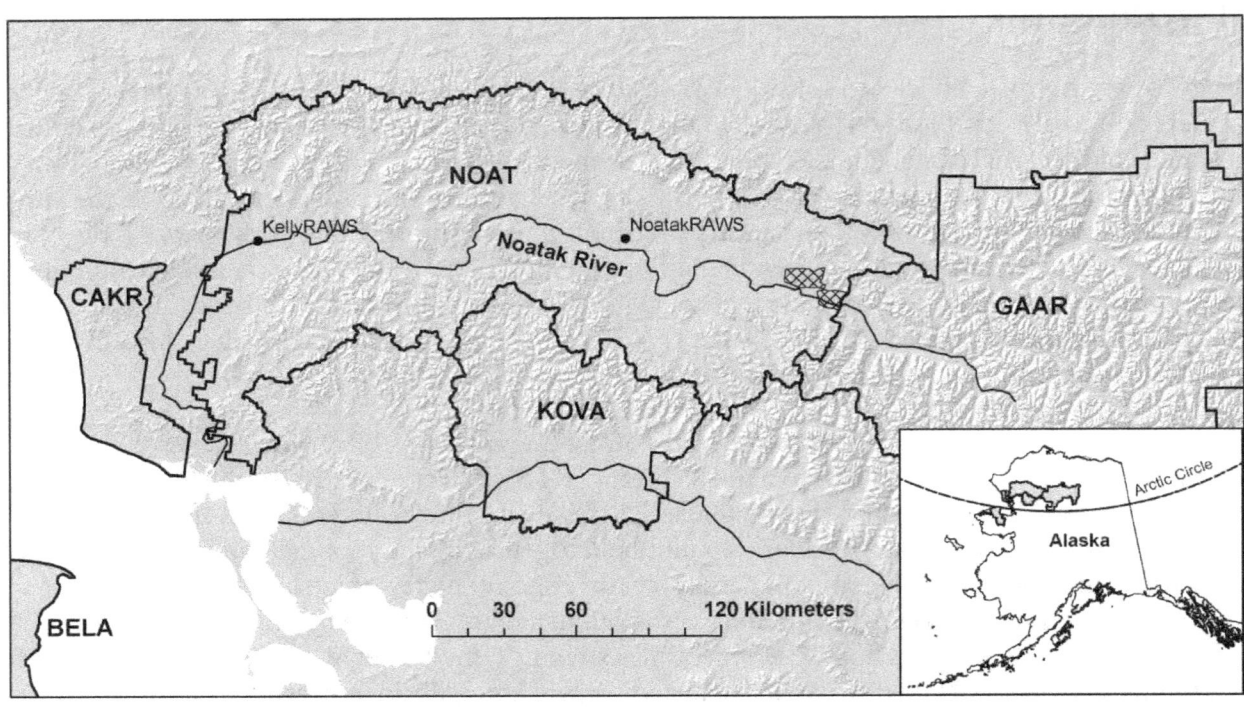

Figure 1. Location of the Noatak National Preserve (NOAT). Other nearby NPS units are also shown: BELA - Bering Land Bridge National Preserve, CAKR - Cape Krusenstern National Monument, KOVA - Kobuk Valley National Park, and GAAR – Gates of the Arctic National Park and Preserve. These 5 NPS units make up the Arctic Inventory and Monitoring Network (ARCN). The hatched area in the eastern part of NOAT is the area where retrogressive thaw slumps were mapped on 1977 aerial photographs, to compare with their 2008 extents on IKONOS imagery.

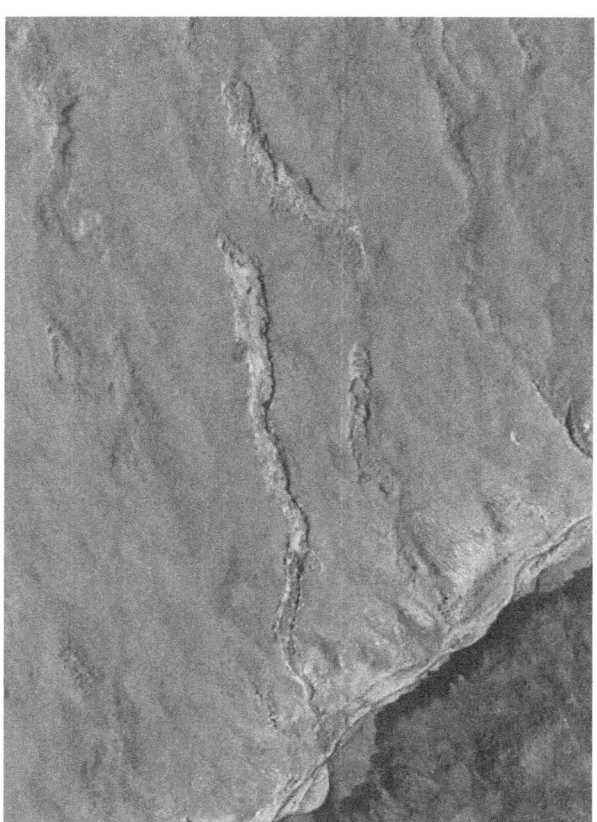

Figure 2. Active-layer detachments (ALD) in the Noatak National Preserve (latitude 68.251°, longitude -157.904°). The grayish strips on this photograph are bare soil exposed by downhill sliding of the vegetation and an approximately 1-m thick layer of thawed soil over permafrost. The largest ALD pictured is about 300 m long and 25 m wide.

Figure 3. A retrogressive thaw slump in the Noatak National Preserve (latitude 67° 48.39', longitude 156° 40.90'). The gray area of mostly bare soil exposed by this slump is about 100 m by 200 m, and the escarpment at the top is about 10 m high. A small residual snow bank is visible near the center of the escarpment (21 June 2010 photo). The smooth, near vertical face just to the left of the snow is a large Pleistocene ice wedge.

Methods

Study Area

The study area is the Noatak National Preserve (NOAT), which covers most of the Noatak River watershed (Fig. 1). NOAT encompasses an intermontane basin in the Brooks Range of northern Alaska, surrounded by rugged mountains with elevations of 1000 to 1500 m. Bedrock lithologies in the study area include a variety of sedimentary, igneous, and metamorphic rocks, with clastic sedimentary rocks being the most widespread (Beikman, 1980). Most of NOAT was glaciated or covered by large ice-dammed lakes in the late Pleistocene (Hamilton, 2001, 2010). Glacial moraines and lake sediments dominate in the lowlands.

NOAT lies within the continuous permafrost zone, where permafrost covers 90% or more of the landscape (Jorgenson et al., 2008). The permafrost is ice-rich and subject to thermokarst in lowland areas throughout the study area, while ice contents are negligible in high mountain areas where bedrock is near the surface. Massive ground ice observed in thaw-slump escarpments includes wedge ice (both small Holocene wedges and larger Pleistocene wedges) and relict glacial ice that has persisted since the end of the Pleistocene (Swanson and Hill, 2010; Swanson, 2012). Glacial moraines that contain relict glacial ice are highly susceptible to thaw slumping (Balser et al., 2006; Swanson and Hill, 2010; Swanson, 2012).

Vegetation in the study area is dominantly arctic tundra, with trees occurring at low elevations, mostly on river floodplains and in the western part of the Preserve. Data from the Noatak RAWS shows a January mean temperature of -25.3 °C, July mean of 13.3 °C, and annual mean of -7.9 °C (WRCC, 2011; for the period 1990-2011 with occasional missing values, mainly in the winter). This station is in the east-central part of the Preserve, in an area of tundra vegetation (Fig. 1). At the Kelly RAWS, the Jan mean is -18.5 °C, July 13.9 °C, annual -4.1 °C (WRCC, 2011; for the period 1990-2011 with winter months largely missing prior to 1998). The Kelly RAWS is in the far western part of the Preserve, in a low-elevation forested area (Fig. 1).

Mapping Methods

Erosion features were mapped by a partially automated process involving both machine processing and visual interpretation of high-resolution imagery The automated process utilized the unique spectral properties of exposed bare soil areas surrounded by vegetation to rapidly delineate unvegetated areas, while visual interpretation was used to take advantage of the human eye's ability to rapidly and accurately differentiate ALD and RTS from other areas of exposed bare soil such as river gravel bars. This process is described in greater detail below.

Exposed bare soil areas originating from active-layer detachments and retrogressive thaw slumps were mapped for the entire Preserve on IKONOS multispectral satellite imagery, (Geoeye, 2010). This imagery includes blue, green, red and near-infrared spectral bands with 4 m resolution, pan-sharpened to 1 m resolution. The images examined were from the snow-free period (late June through early October) of 2006, 2007, and 2008. Mapping was incomplete in some areas due to cloud cover. Images were orthorectified with the best available digital elevation model, the National Elevation Dataset at 60 m resolution (USGS, 2006), and projected to the Alaska Albers projection.

Erosion features were mapped by a 3-step process: 1) digitize bare-soil polygons by automated process, 2) manually create a point layer marking all thaw-related erosion features visible on imagery, with the feature type as an attribute, and 3) join these two layers to extract permafrost-related bare soils areas and eliminate non-target bare soil areas (such as river gravel bars), and transfer the erosion-feature type information to the polygons (Fig. 4).

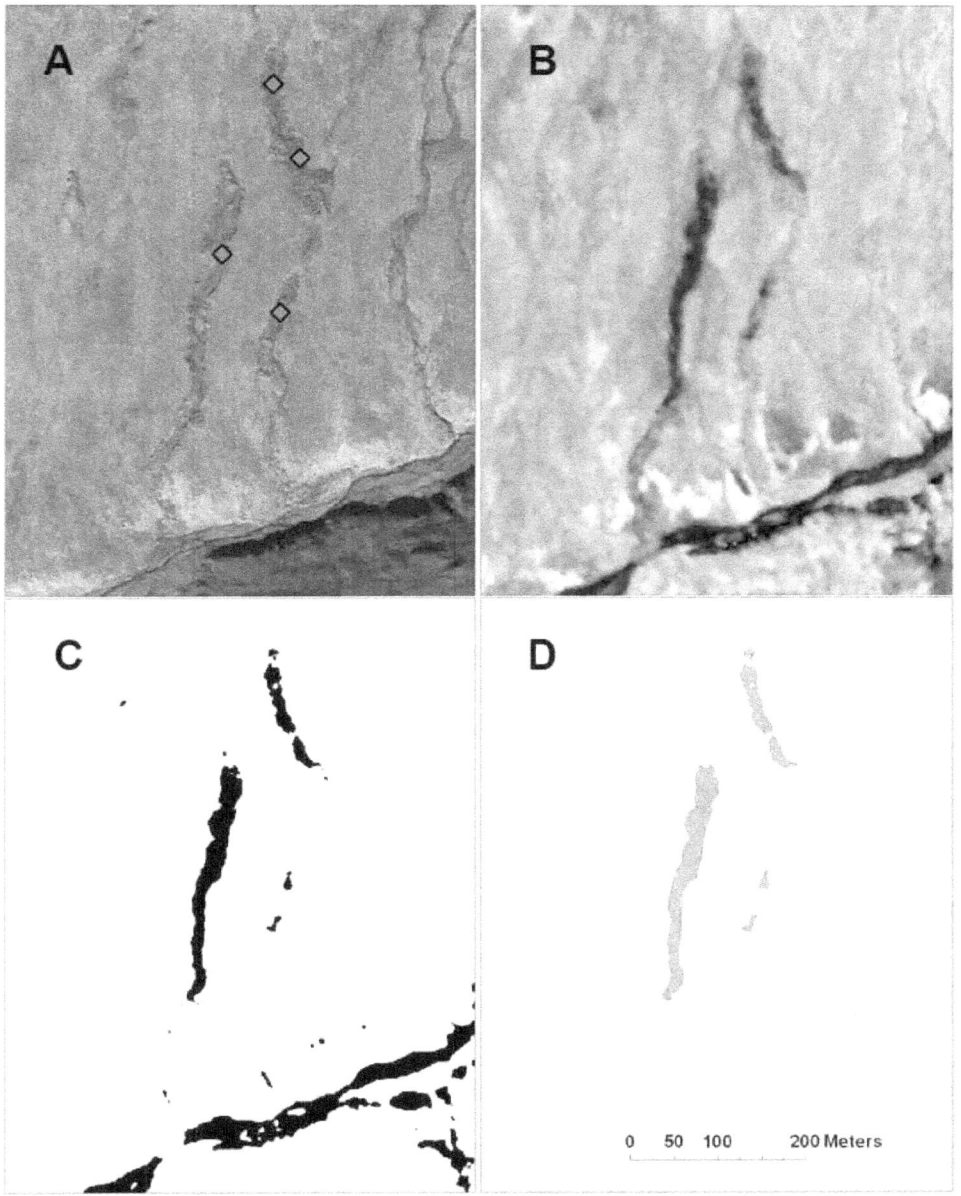

Figure 4. Mapping of the erosion features in Fig. 2. A) IKONOS image with color-infrared color scheme and ALD marked with points. B) NDVI of the IKONOS image. C) NDVI image thresholded to differentiate bare soil (black) from vegetated areas (white). D) Polygons produced by conversion of the thresholded image to a polygon layer and intersection with points in (A). (Latitude 68.25°, longitude -157.90°.)

Delineation of bare-soil polygons

First, the normalized difference vegetation index (NDVI) was computed from the near infrared (NIR) and red spectral bands of the IKONOS images. NDVI is a measure of "greenness" that is closely related to leaf area and biomass (Tucker and Sellers, 1986). NDVI is (NIR - red)/(NIR + red). It is high (near 1) in densely vegetated areas and zero or lower in unvegetated areas. A median filter using a circle with a radius of 3 pixels was then applied to the NDVI image, to reduce speckling in the images while preserving features greater than 10 m across. The median filter passed the circular window across the NDVI image, at each position computed the median value of all pixels within the circle, and assigned the median to the center pixel. Next, a threshold NDVI value was chosen for each image to separate vegetated and unvegetated areas; this value was usually between 0 and -0.1 for the various images. In practice, this threshold value was chosen during the next step, visual identification of erosion features. Finally, the unvegetated areas (with NDVI below the threshold) were converted from raster (pixel) format to polygons (line-delineated).

Identification of permafrost-related erosion features

The point layer of permafrost-related erosion features was produced by systematic examination of the images. Images were displayed in the color scheme of color-infrared aerial photographs to enhance visibility of unvegetated areas. A grid with 4 by 4 km cells was placed over each image, and each cell in the grid was searched at 1:20,000 scale for any potential erosion features, which were then examined at a larger scale (1:5,000 or larger) to verify and label them as ALD or RTS. The NDVI image was turned on and off over the color-infra-red image to help locate bare-soil areas and determine the appropriate NDVI threshold value to use for mapping bare-soil areas as described above. Features with 2 or more disjunct patches of bare soil that were part of a single feature (e.g., an ALD with a block of vegetation that slid partway down and separated the bare soil into two patches) were given multiple points with the same identifying number. The ecological subsection (Jorgenson et al., 2001) of each feature was also added as an attribute.

Active-layer detachments produce strips of bare soil 10 to 30 m wide and up to hundreds of meters long on slopes; they stand in sharp contrast to adjacent, densely vegetated areas. ALD are distinguished from other bare soil areas by their shape, the presence of a deformed soil-vegetation mat at their downhill end, and orientation vertically up and down a slope. Features readily confused with ALD include: 1) elongate snow beds (which lack the deformed vegetation-soil mat, are often oriented across the slope, and often have a snow patch in summer images); 2) elongated eroded areas along small streams (which also lack the deformed vegetation mat, typically have pointed as opposed to blunt ends, and have a stream entering and exiting from their upper and lower ends); and 3) elongate patches of scree or rubble, which again lack the deformed vegetation-soil mat and typically occur in a pattern related to bedrock outcrops.

The features of RTS that distinguish them from other unvegetated areas include: 1) generally equant shape with an escarpment along part of the perimeter, 2) location on slopes with fine-grained geologic materials (as opposed to terrain with coarse rubble or exposed bedrock), 3) evidence for transport of significant sediment from the RTS, in the form of an evacuation channel or debris fan (Lacelle et al., 2010). Many RTS occur along a river or lakeshore bluff that provided the initial exposure of ice to thaw. RTS were sometimes difficult to differentiate from barren slopes of river bluffs. In the absence of thaw slumping, a bare area on the river bluff is expected to be a simple slope near angle of repose (or steeper in consolidated material) that ends abruptly at the floodplain where material is removed by fluvial erosion. RTS were identified in these settings if the escarpment had retreated back, usually developing a curved form with a steep scarp and gentler floor (Fig. 5).

Figure 5. (Left) Retrogressive thaw slump on a Noatak river bluff (latitude 68.0° 04.22' longitude 159° 14.65'). Steep slopes (1) represent riverbank erosion of weakly consolidated sediment without significant thaw slumping. A retrogressive thaw slump (2) has grown inland from the top of the bluff, producing a steep escarpment above a gentler floor area. (Right) Oblique aerial photograph close-up of the slump.

Spatial join of polygon and point layers

Bare-soil polygons that either contained a thaw-feature point within them, or had a point fall within 20 m of their boundaries were identified by automated process and given the attributes of the point. All other bare-soil polygons were deleted. This spatial join eliminated the numerous bare polygons of other origins, such as river sandbars and bedrock outcrops. The resulting polygons were inspected and edited as needed, most often to remove unwanted areas (e.g., a river gravel bar that was contiguous with a slump and was joined with it into one polygon.) The area of each ALD or RTS was then computed; these areas do not include the displaced vegetated mats typically present at the lower end of an ALD.

Analysis of Environmental Factors

The relationship of the erosion features to topographic slope and aspect were determined by overlay of the erosion feature polygons (e.g., Fig. 4D) onto slope and aspect raster maps. The slope and aspect rasters were derived by the NPS Alaska Regional Office from the 60 m National Elevation Dataset (NED) digital elevation model (DEM); the 60 m NED DEM raster was re-sampled to 30 m using cubic convolution (i.e., smoothed) before computation of slope and aspect. The erosion feature polygons can be small relative to the NED DEM raster pixels. To deal with this problem, the erosion feature polygons were converted to a 5 m raster, and the slope raster, and aspect raster were re-sampled to a 5 m pixel size by the "nearest neighbor" method (i.e., without any additional interpolation) before the analysis. As a result of the coarseness of the DEM, the slopes and aspects associated with any given erosion feature include data derived from a neighborhood up to several 10s of meters outside its boundaries, which probably increases variability but should have minor effects on the mean for ALD or RTS as a whole. Also, since the slope and aspect of each pixel in an erosion feature was used to compute summary statistics for all features, the results are weighted by size of the features.

The relationship of erosion features to surficial geology and ecological unit (subsection) were determined by overlay of feature center points onto maps by Hamilton (2010) and Jorgenson et al. (2001).

Mapping on Historical Images

Areas of bare soil due to retrogressive thaw slumping were also mapped for a selected area on scanned aerial photography, AHAP color-infrared images from 17 July 1977 (Fig. 1). This area was chosen using the map of RTS in NOAT made from IKONOS imagery: it contains the greatest concentration of classic RTS in the Preserve, many of which are the subject of detailed monitoring (Swanson and Hill, 2010; Swanson, 2012). Scans of the aerial photographs were made by the US Geological Survey and included green, red, and near-infrared bands, allowing computation of NDVI. Four photos were needed to cover the study area. Two photos had scan resolutions of 0.8 m and the other two had scan resolutions of 1.5 m. This disparity was not ideal, but the resulting polygons on all photos were judged to be comparable to those obtained from the 1-m resolution IKONOS imagery. Bare soil polygons were digitized on the raw scanned photo images by the same method as described above for the IKONOS images, and the area of the polygons was summed in uncalibrated pixel units. The photos were georeferenced to the IKONOS images using a first-order (affine) transformation, and the scale terms from the transformations were used to convert the polygon areas on the photos from pixels units to square meters. Visual overlay of the georeferenced photos onto the IKONOS images revealed very little distortion of the photo-derived polygons, thanks to the photos' high-altitude (1:60,000 scale), the gentle relief of the study area, and choice of polygons from overlapping photos such that the version nearest the photo center was used.

Results

Active-Layer Detachments

A total of 848 active-layer detachments were located in the Preserve, exposing a total area of 103 ha of bare soil (Fig. 6). ALD ranged in size from nearly 3 ha of exposed bare soil (Fig. 7) to just a few tens of square meters. ALD were distributed unevenly, with high concentrations in the vegetated hills and rounded mountains composed mostly of sedimentary rock in the southwestern and northeastern parts of the Preserve (Fig. 6). ALD were rare in the lowlands, where appropriate slopes are generally lacking, except locally on river bluffs. They were also rare in rugged high-mountain areas with abundant exposed bedrock (visible as white or gray tones in Fig. 6). ALD were rare in some terrain in the Preserve that appears suitable for them: note the few ALD in vegetated hilly areas in the north-central, northwestern, and southeastern parts of the Preserve (Fig. 6).

The occurrence of ALD on specific physiographic land types is demonstrated by a strong link between ALD and Ecological Subsections (Jorgenson et al., 2001). Seven subsections had a density of over 50 ALD per thousand square kilometers. These seven subsections covered just 20% of the Preserve but contained 86% of the ALD (Fig. 8). These subsections are all described as mountains or hills composed of non-carbonate, sedimentary rocks.

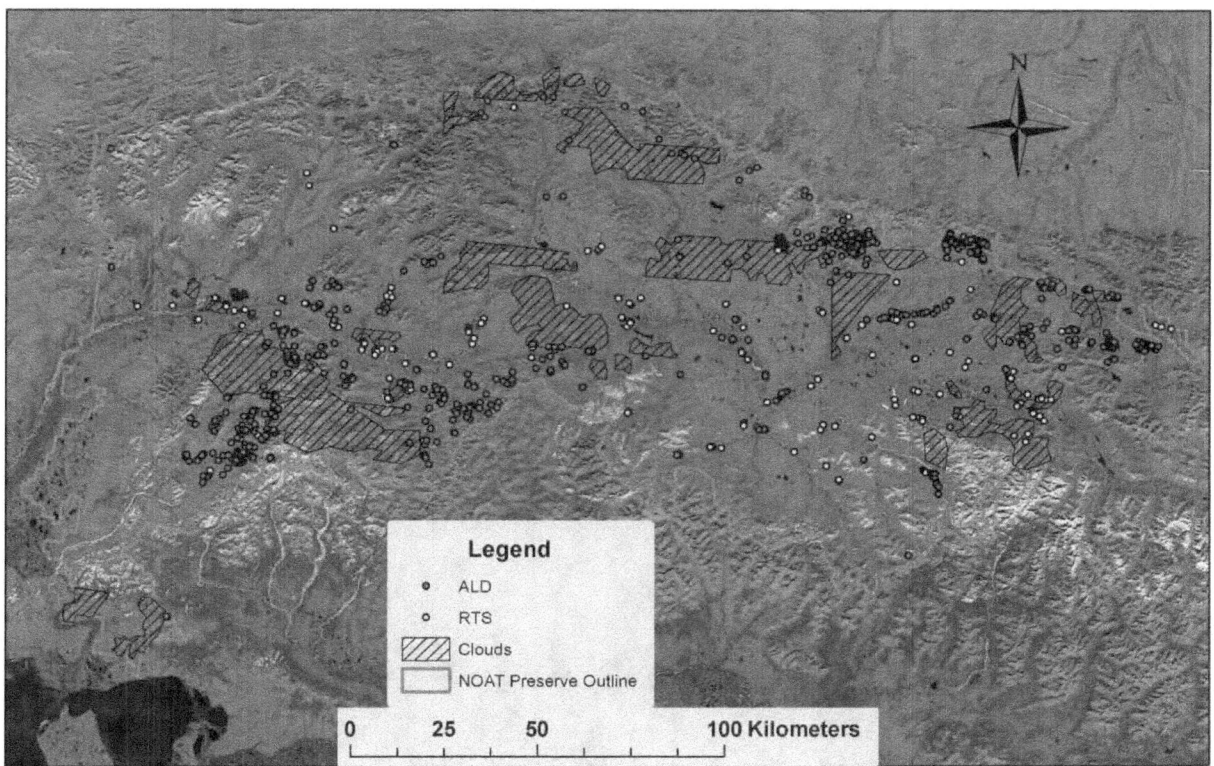

Figure 6. Active-layer detachments (ALD) and retrogressive thaw slumps (RTS) in the Noatak National Preserve, mapped from 2006-2008 IKONOS satellite imagery. Hatched areas show where clouds and cloud shadows obscured or partly obscured the ground and prevented accurate mapping.

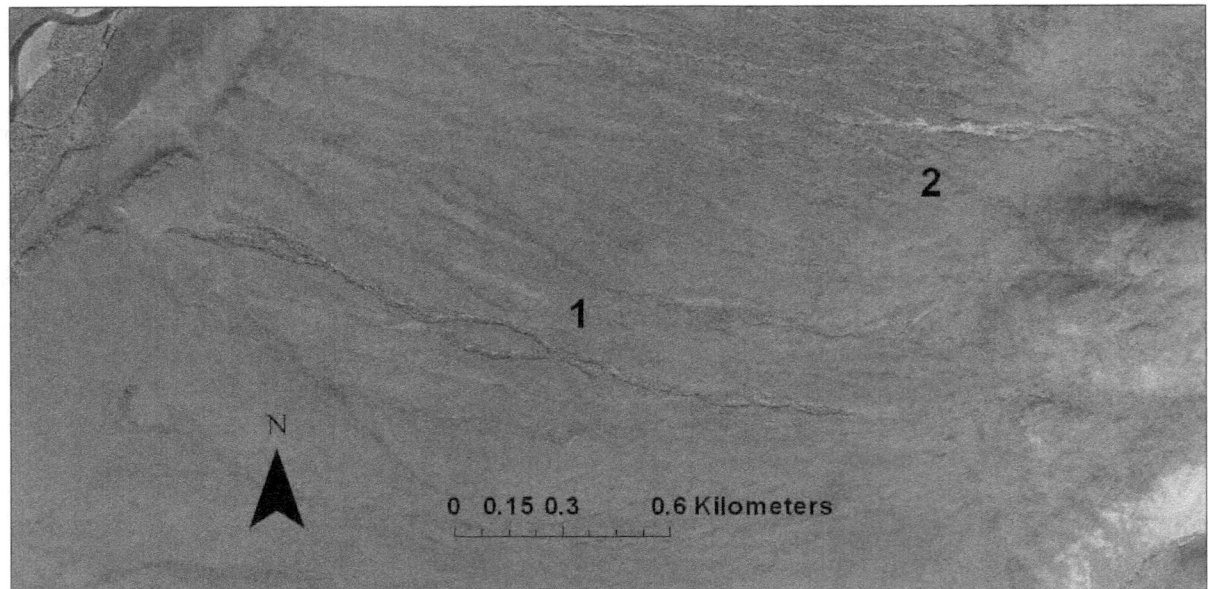

Figure 7. Example of large active-layer detachments in Noatak National Preserve. ALD (1) was approximately 2 km long in 2007 and exposed nearly 3 ha of bare soil. This feature slopes to the west-northwest, with a gradient ranging from 13% in the upper part to about 7% in the lower part. A nearby ALD (2) was about 700 m long and exposed over 2 ha of bare soil. They are on the lower slopes of the Isacheluich Mountains above the Kaluktavik River, a tributary of the Noatak River, near 68.0° N, 160.82° W.

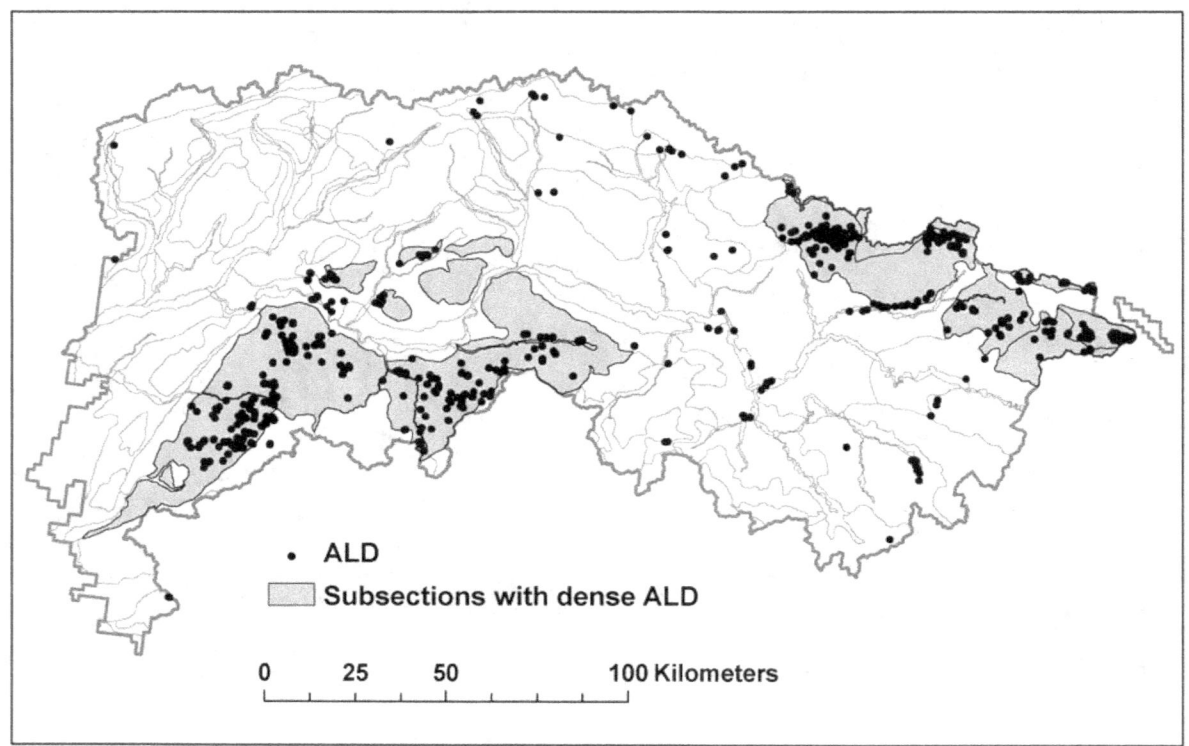

Figure 8. Ecological subsections with dense occurrence of ALD in Noatak National Preserve. Shaded gray are the seven ecological subsections (Jorgenson et al., 2001) with more than 50 ALD per 1000 square kilometers.

The mean surface slope for ALD polygons as measured by GIS analysis was 16%, (median 14%) and the standard deviation was 8%. This standard deviation is probably wider than the variation in slope on ALD that would be measured on the ground as a result of the coarseness of the DEM and registration errors. ALD were most common on southwest-facing slopes and least common on east-facing slopes (Fig. 9).

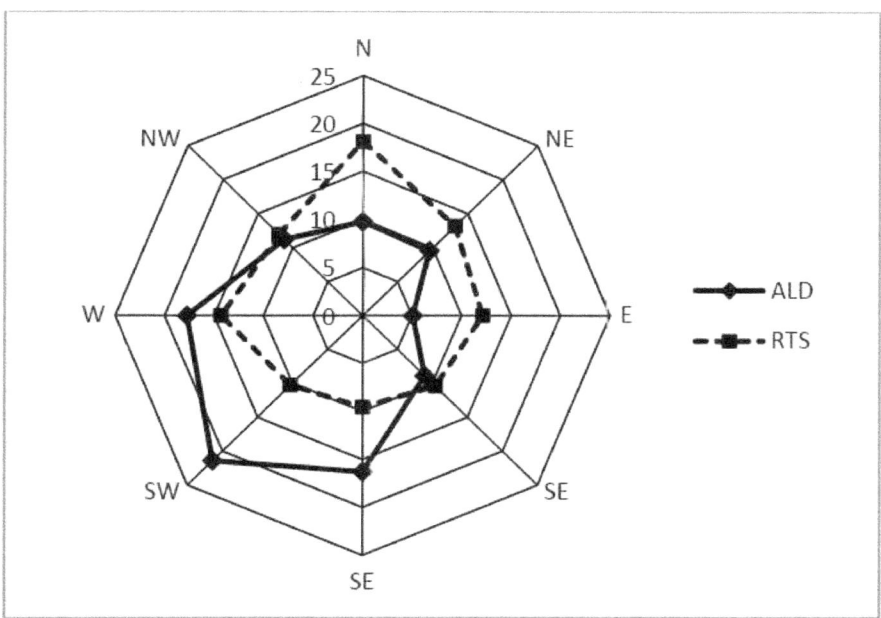

Figure 9. Slope aspect of ALD and RTS in Noatak National Preserve. ALD and RTS polygons were overlaid on a raster layer of aspect in degrees with 30 m resolution. The diagram shows the percent of pixels in ALD and RTS that fell into aspect classes representing cardinal directions (N – north, 337.5 to 22.5°; NE – northeast, 22.5 to 67.5°; E – east, 67.5 to 112.5°, etc.).

Retrogressive Thaw Slumps

A total of 276 retrogressive thaw slumps were identified (Fig. 6). They ranged in size from about 4 ha of exposed bare soil (Fig. 10) to a few tens of square meters. RTS exposed a total area of 90 ha of bare soil in NOAT. They were distributed unevenly in the preserve (Fig. 6). The common settings for RTS in the Preserve were as follows:

On bluffs along major rivers (n = 101). Most of these RTS were along the Noatak River (n = 75), in areas mapped as glacial till and glacial lake deposits of various ages; the most common was glacial lake deposits of Avan age (last glacial maximum, 11,000-24,000 yr B.P.). Few slumps occurred along other major rivers except the Aniuk river, where a swarm of about 15 slumps was found in a single 4-km stretch, in an area mapped by Hamilton (2010) as glacial lake deposits over Sagavanirktok glacial till (middle Pleistocene, between 130,000 and 780,000 yr B.P.; Hamilton, 2009).

Along lake shores (n = 80). The most common geological materials where RTS occurred along lake shores were late Pleistocene glacial tills of Avan (last glacial maximum, 11,000-24,000 yr B.P.), Anisak (early Wisconsin, approximately 60,000 to 100,000 yr B.P.), and Makpik (late interglacial, approximately 100,000 yr B.P.) age. Glacial lake deposits, and glacial lake deposits over Anisak glacial till were also represented.

Along creeks (n = 38). These RTS were also mainly in glacial till, of Cutler (middle Pleistocene,) and Makpik (late interglacial) age, plus some in glacial lake sediments.

On upland slopes away from water bodies (n = 58). These RTS were mostly on glacial till, representing a wide range of glaciations from the Cutler (middle to early Pleistocene) to Makpik, Anisak, and Avan (late Pleistocene). Some were also on glacial lake or solifluction deposits. An interesting group of upland RTS occurred in the Baird Mountains (the southwestern-most cluster visible in Fig. 6) in an area mapped as silt-covered bedrock by Hamilton (2010).

The correspondence between RTS and subsections is not as clear as it is for ALD; they are distributed across a number of subsections where deep Pleistocene sediments are found. The most striking coincidence of RTS and subsection is for the Kavachurak Glaciated Uplands subsection (Fig. 11), which consists mostly of Pleistocene glacial moraine near the Noatak River in far eastern NOAT. This subsection has the highest density of RTS in NOAT, both in terms of the number of RTS and area occupied by RTS.

The mean slope of RTS, as measured by GIS analysis, was 12% (median 11%) with a standard deviation of 9%. Again the standard deviation was probably exaggerated over what would be measured on the ground, due to registration errors and the coarseness of the DEM. RTS were most common on north-facing slopes and least common on south-facing slopes (Fig. 9)

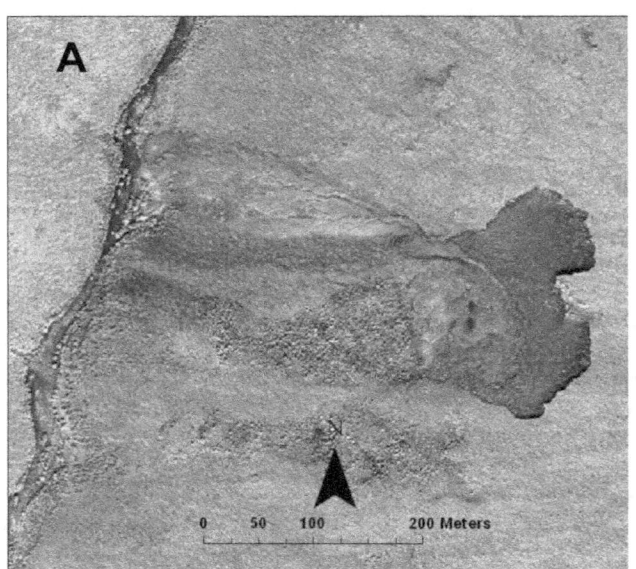 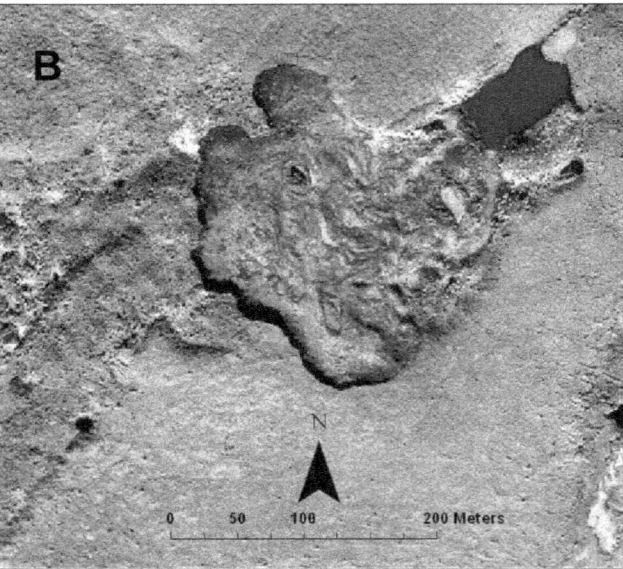

Figure 10. Examples of large retrogressive thaw slumps exposing about 4 ha of bare soil. Slump (A) was expanding uphill to the east and had shed material down a large alluvial fan to a nearby creek. Slump (B) was expanding along a prominent scarp to the south and west. These two slumps are portrayed in detail in Swanson and Hill (2010) and Swanson (2012; slumps NOAT070 and NOAT151).

Historical change in retrogressive thaw slumps: 1977 vs. 2008

In the study area analyzed for historical change (about 190 square kilometers; Fig. 11), I identified 23 RTS, covering a total of 13.5 ha, on AHAP color-infrared imagery from 17 July 1977. On IKONOS imagery from 9 Aug 2008 I identified 35 RTS covering 21.2 ha. This increase was recorded in spite of some cloud cover on the 2008 imagery that may have led me to miss some slumps for the later date. All of the slumps active in 1977 were still visible as revegetated scars on the 2008 imagery (Fig 12). The RTS active in 2008 were mostly in places that were undisturbed in 1977, though a few appear to originate from reactivated or expanded 1977 slumps (Fig. 12).

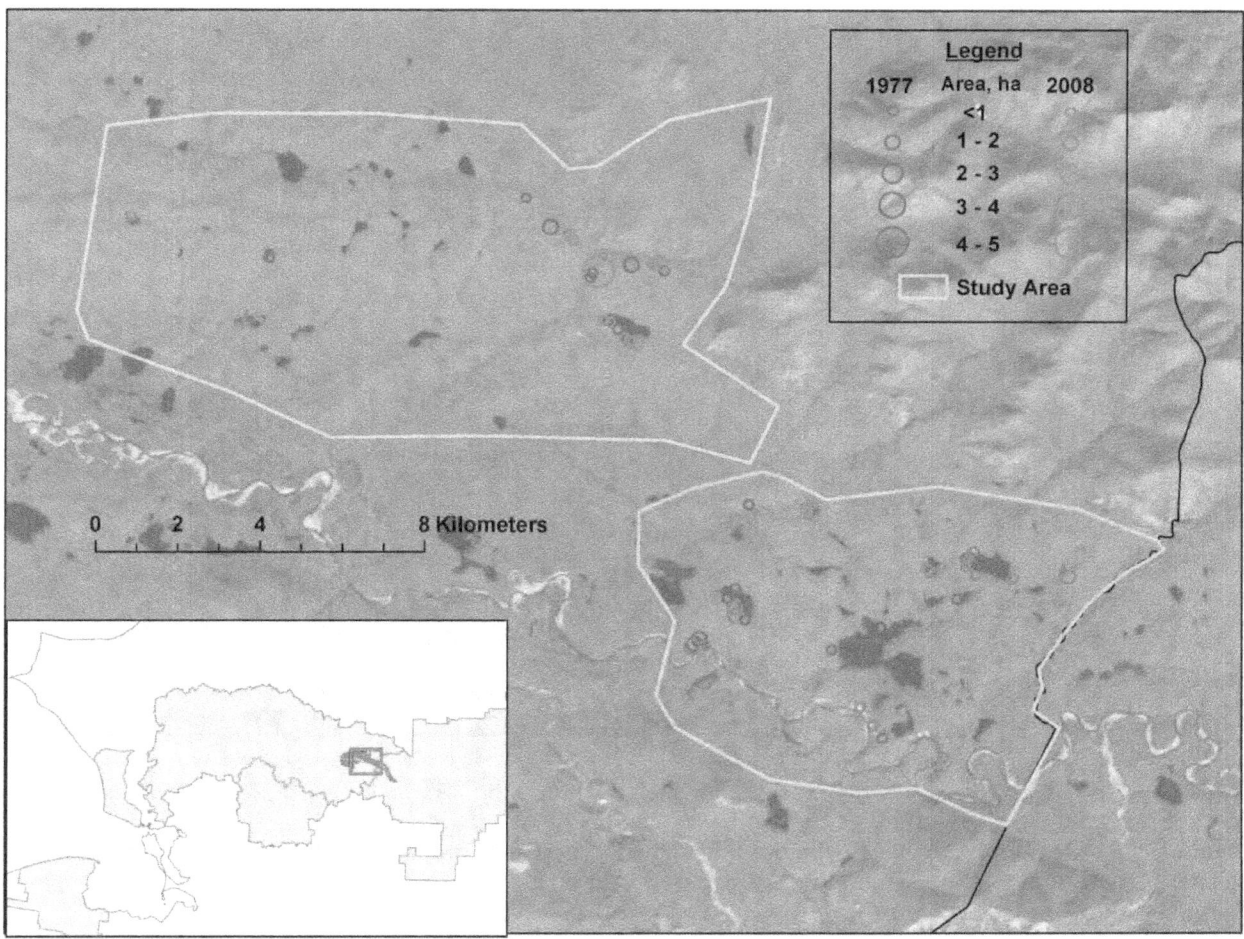

Figure 11. Comparison of retrogressive thaw slumps in 1977 and 2009 in a part of the Kavachurak Glaciated Uplands Subsection. (The subsection is shown in blue on the inset map, and the area of the main map is outlined there in red.) Slumps are symbclized by circles sized proportional to the area of bare soil exposed. Slumps were mapped using AHAP color-infrared aerial photographs in 1977 (blue circles) and IKONOS satellite imagery in 2008 (red circles). Between 1977 and 2008 the total number of slumps increased from 23 to 35 and total area of exposed bare soil increased from 13.5 to 21.2 ha.

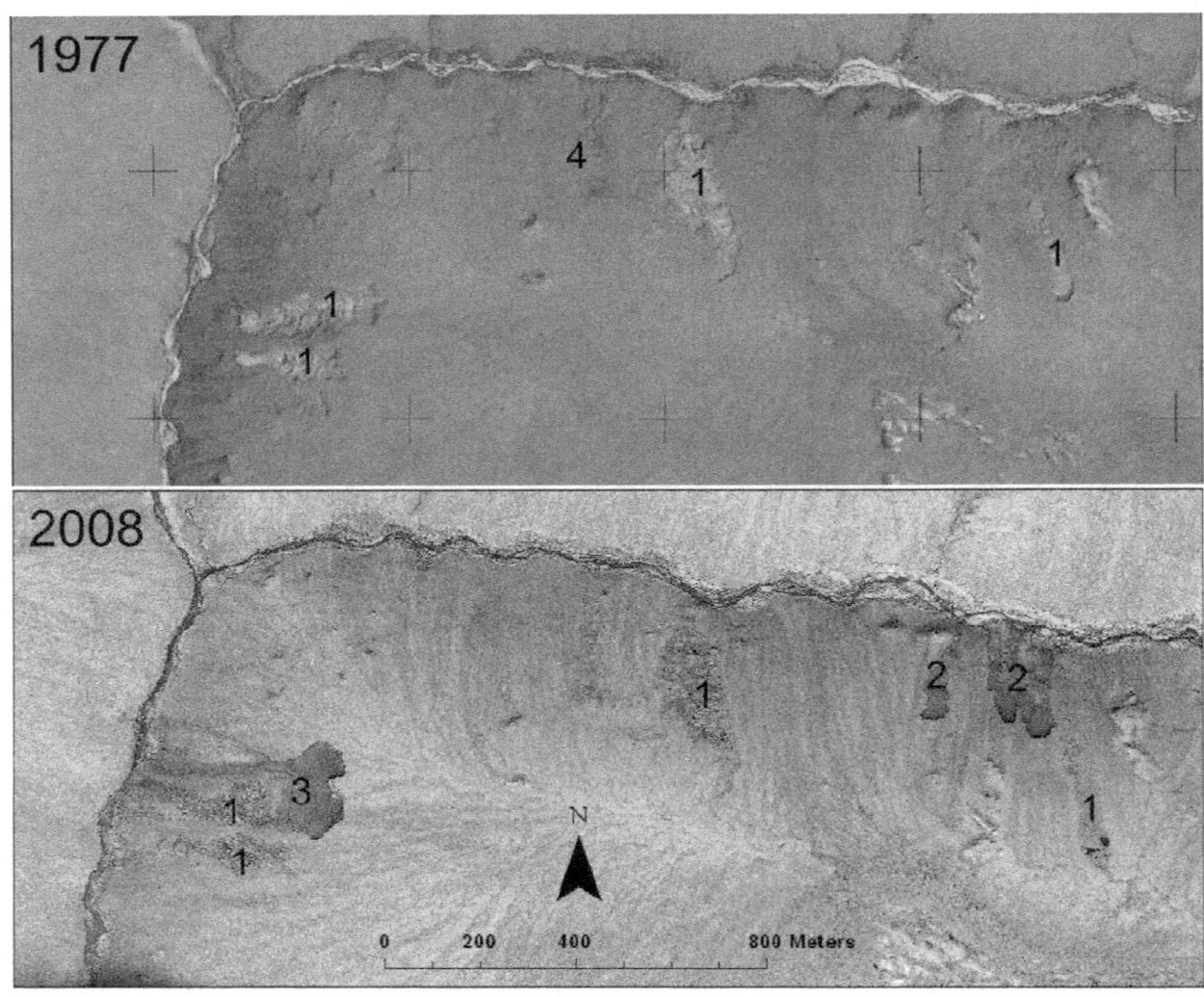

Figure 12. Example retrogressive thaw slumps in 1977 and 2008. The slumps present in 1977 (labeled 1 on both images) stabilized and revegetated with little additional growth after 1977. The currently active slumps at (2) developed in places without any activity in 1977. Active slump (3) reactivated and expanded a slump present in 1977. A revegetated slump is visible on the 1977 imagery (4).

14

Discussion and Conclusions

Active-layer detachments

ALD formation requires both suitable site conditions and a climatic trigger event consisting of warm summer weather, possibly augmented by rainfall (Carter and Galloway, 1981; Lewkowicz and Harris, 2005). Weather data from the Kelly and Noatak RAWS, located in the western and east-central parts of NOAT, respectively, show that the summers of 2004 and 2007 were exceptionally warm and could be responsible for the ALD mapped as a part of this study (Fig. 13). ALD require a period of "pre-conditioning" during which ground ice accumulates (Lewkowicz and Harris, 2005), and slopes are more stable for a period of years after a major event because the most susceptible sites have released. Thus if 2004 and 2007 were similar in depth of thaw (Fig. 13), we would expect the former year to have been the more important ALD event. Areas of overlap between images from the different years (2006-2008) that were examined as a part of the mapping process showed essentially no changes during this period, suggesting that indeed the main event was in 2004 rather than 2007.

Re-vegetation of some ALD was apparent on satellite imagery (Fig. 14). Informal observations of ALD by the author in NOAT in 2010 and 2011 gave the distinct impression that ALD were re-vegetating, or, in some cases, continuing to erode by flowing surface water, but fresh detachments were not observed. The episodic nature of ALD and their re-vegetation within a matter of years presents problems for monitoring. Retrospective study of ALD frequency using historical imagery will be difficult in ARCN because we have just two early image dates for most of our region: early 1950s (incomplete coverage) and approximately 1980. If the formation of ALD is episodic and infrequent, and revegetation makes them difficult to map after just 5 to 10 years, then we are likely to miss events using historical photography. Monitoring methods for the future are the subject of ongoing research (Balser et al., 2010).

The lack of ALD in the gentle mountain areas in the northwestern, north-central, and southeastern parts of NOAT may reflect some geological factor or locally less severe warming in 2004 and 2007. Continued observation of these areas in the future is recommended, in spite of their apparent lack of susceptibility to detachments.

The abundance of ALD on west-southwest slope aspects suggests that these aspects react more strongly to exceptionally warm summers, allowing thaw of the ice-rich material at the base of the active layer. In the continuous permafrost zone of NOAT, an ice-rich layer in the upper permafrost is presumably available on any aspect. In contrast to my study, Lewkowicz and Harris (2005) found more ALD on north-facing slopes in the forested Mackenzie Valley. Their study area was in the discontinuous permafrost zone where south-facing slopes lack permafrost or have ice-poor permafrost.

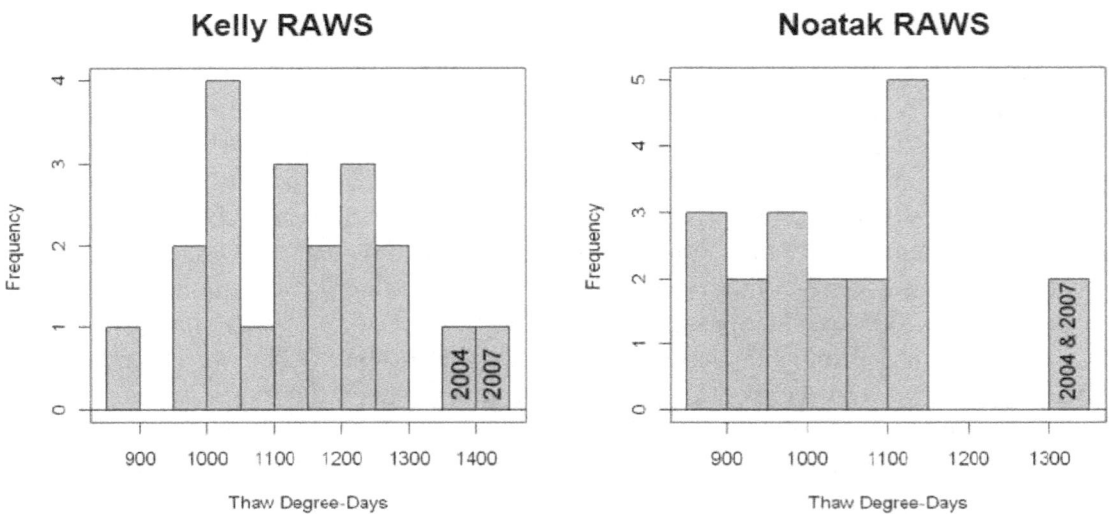

Figure 13. Frequency of annual thaw degree-days in °C at the Kelly (1990-2010 missing 1996) and Noatak (1992-2010) RAWS weather stations. The exceptionally warm summers of 2004 and 2007 are noted. Thaw degree-days were estimated from June, July, and August mean temperatures by summing the number of days in the month times the monthly mean temperature in °C.

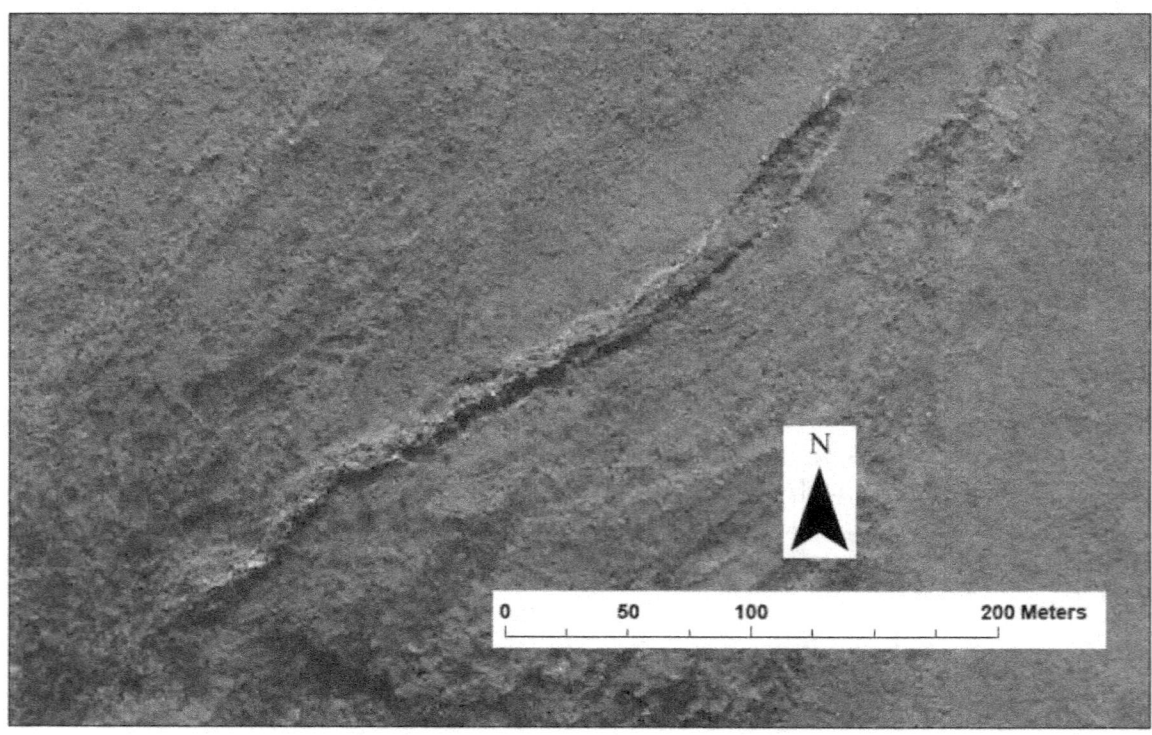

Figure 14. Example of a revegetating ALD (NOAT252) on IKONOS imagery from 14 September 2008. Little of this ALD is still exposed bare soil, except in the channel that is apparently continuing to erode by running water.

Retrogressive Thaw Slumps

Examination of exposures of sediment and ground ice in 13 RTS in NOAT by Swanson and Hill, (2010) and Swanson (2012) showed them to be exclusively on glacial till deposits, and glacial ice was present in many main scarp exposures. Mackay and Dallimore (1992) refuted the glacial origin of massive ground ice in glacial tills of northwestern Canada, and scientists there have searched for non-glacial explanations for the ice causing RTS in these tills (Lacelle et al., 2004). However, more recent work in northwestern Canada by Murton et al. (2005) has supported a glacial origin for massive tabular ice bodies under till, similar to what we observed in NOAT.

Glacial till deposits are widespread in NOAT (Hamilton, 2010) and, owing to their location in the continuous permafrost zone, these tills may conceal relict glacial ice in many places. Thus in NOAT, glacial till deposits may be used to predict where relict glacial ice masses could be present and thaw slumping more likely. Fine-grained lacustrine deposits or glacial tills could also contain enough ground ice of other origin (e.g., ice wedges and segregated ice) to produce RTS.

The relict Pleistocene glacial ice that we see in NOAT is typically preserved under a meter or two of dominantly fine-grained material containing occasional cobbles and boulders (Swanson and Hill, 2010; Swanson 2012). This relatively fine-grained till overburden probably originates mainly from subglacial debris entrained into basal glacial ice (Hubbard et al., 2009). The glaciers incorporated sediment (potentially including till, alluvium, loess, and lacustrine sediment) into the basal ice, where freezing and deformation mixed it with cleaner ice. Then ablation of the ice eventually brought these basal sediments on top of the remaining ice. If the glacial ice contained enough debris to allow a meter or two of dominantly fine-grained sediment to accumulate on the surface through ablation, the superglacial debris layer would be thicker than typical active layers in fine-grained sediments and any remaining glacial ice would be preserved in permafrost.

The fact that RTS occur preferentially on north-facing slopes is perhaps counter-intuitive, as we might expect them, like ALD, to occur on warm slopes where ice is more likely to thaw. Perhaps the large ice bodies required for RTS (e.g., Pleistocene glacial and wedge ice) has not been preserved on some south-facing aspects. Kokelj et al. (2009) also found RTS to be most common on north-facing slopes in northwestern Canada.

Comparison of 2008 and 1977 RTS in a selected area suggests that slumping is more widespread today than it was a few decades ago. A likely explanation is that the abrupt climatic warming in Alaska after 1976 (Hartmann and Wendler, 2005) has caused permafrost warming and accelerated thermokarst activity (Osterkamp and Romanovsky, 1999; Jorgenson et al., 2006). RTS also increased in area from 1970 to the 2000s in the Mackenzie River Valley (Lantz and Kokelj (2008) and on Herschel Island (Lantuit and Pollard, 2008) in northwestern Canada.

Literature Cited

Balser, A. W., M. N. Gooseff, J. B. Jones, W. B. Bowden, D. M. Sanzone, A. Allen, and J. R. Larouche. 2006. Thermokarst characteristics and distribution in a transitional arctic biome: new discoveries and possible monitoring directions in a climate change scenario. American Geophysical Union, Fall Meeting 2006, abstract #C51B-0428.

Balser, A. W. W. B. Bowden, J. B. Jones, M. N. Gooseff, D. M. Sanzone, A. Bouchier, and A. Allen. 2007. Thermokarst distribution in the Noatak Basin, Alaska: increased frequency and correlations with local and regional landscape variables. American Geophysical Union, Fall Meeting 2007, abstract #C32A-08.

Balser, A., J. B. Jones, and T. Jorgenson. 2010. Thermokarst Associations with Landscape Characteristics in Arctic Alaska: Implications for Future Permafrost Degradation at Landscape to Regional Scales. American Geophysical Union, Fall Meeting 2010, abstract #C31A-0501.

Beikman, H. M. 1980. Geologic Map of Alaska. Miscellaneous Geologic Investigations Map I-357 1 US Geological Survey (Scale 1:1,584,000).

Bowden, S. B., M. N. Gooseff, A. Balser, A. Green, B. J. Peterson, and J. Bradford. 2008. Sediment and nutrient delivery from thermokarst features in the foothills of the North Slope, Alaska: Potential impact on headwater stream ecosystems. Journal of Geophysical Research 113, G02026, doi:10.1029/2007JG000470,2008.

Burn, C. R., and A. G. Lewkowicz. 1990. Retrogressive thaw slumps. Canadian landform examples – 17. The Canadian Geographer 34(3):273–276.

Carter, L. D., and J. P. Galloway. 1981. Earth flows along Henry Creek, Northern Alaska. Arctic, 34, 325-328.

Crosby, B. T. 2009. Progressive Growth, Modulated Supply: How coupling and decoupling between an enormous retrogressive thaw slump and its depositional fan impacts sediment delivery to the Selawik River, Northwest Alaska. American Geophysical Union, Fall Meeting 2009, Abstract U41C-0043.

Geoeye. 2010. Imagery sources. IKONOS. http://www.geoeye.com/CorpSite/products/imagery-sources/Default.aspx. Accessed 1 March 2010.

Hamilton, T. D. 2001. Quaternary glacial, lacustrine, and fluvial interactions in the western Noatak basin, northwest Alaska. Quaternary Science Reviews 20:371-391.

Hamilton, T. D. 2009. Guide to surficial geology and river-bluff exposures, Noatak National Preserve, northwestern Alaska. U.S. Geological Survey Scientific Investigations Report 2008-5125.

Hamilton, T. D. 2010. Surficial geologic map of the Noatak National Preserve, Alaska. U.S Geological Survey Scientific Investigations Map 3036.

Hartmann, B., and G. Wendler. 2005. The significance of the 1976 Pacific climate shift in the climatology of Alaska. Journal of Climate 18:4824–4839.

Hubbard, B., S. Cook, and H. Coulson. 2009. Basal ice facies: a review and unifying approach. Quaternary Science Reviews 28:1956-1969.

Jorgenson, M. T., D. K. Swanson, and M. Macander. 2001. Landscape-level mapping of ecological units for the Noatak National Preserve, Alaska. Inventory and Monitoring Program, National Park Service, Alaska Region, Anchorage, Alaska.

Jorgenson, M. T., Y. L. Shur, and E. R. Pullman. 2006. Abrupt increase in permafrost degradation in Alaska. Geophysical Research Letters 33:L02503.

Jorgenson, T., K. Yoshikawa, M. Kanevskiy, Y. Shur, V. Romanovsky, S. Marchenko, G. Grosse, J. Brown, and B. Jones. 2008. Permafrost characteristics of Alaska. Proceedings of the Ninth International Conference on Permafrost. University of Alaska Fairbanks, Institute of Northern Engineering. Scale 1:7,200,000

Kokelj, S. V., R. E. Jenkins, D. Milburn, C. R. Burn, and N. Snow. 2005. The influence of thermokarst disturbance on the water quality of small upland lakes, Mackenzie Delta region, Northwest Territories, Canada. Permafrost and Periglacial Processes 16:343-353.

Kokelj, S. V., T. C. Lantz, J. Kanigan, S. L. Smith and R. Coutts. 2009. Origin and polycyclic behavior of tundra thaw slumps, Mackenzie Delta region, Northwest Territories, Canada. Permafrost and Periglacial Processes 20:173–184.

Lacelle, D., J. Bjornson, B. Lauriol, I. D. Clark, and Y. Troutet. 2004. Segregated-intrusive ice of subglacial meltwater origin in retrogressive thaw flow headwalls, Richardson Mountains, NWT, Canada. Quaternary Science Reviews 23(5-6):681-696.

Lacelle, D., J. Bjornson, and B. Lauriol. 2010. Climatic and geomorphic factors affecting contemporary (1950-2004) activity of retrogressive thaw slumps on the Aklavik Plateau, Richardson Mountains, NWT, Canada. Permafrost and Periglacial Processes 21:1–15.

Lamoureaux, S. F., and M. J. Lafrenière. 2009. Fluvial impact of extensive active layer detachments, Cape Boundary, Melville Island, Canada. Arctic, Antarctic, and Alpine Research 41(1):59–68.

Lantuit, H., and W. H. Pollard. 2008. Fifty years of coastal erosion and retrogressive thaw slump activity on Herschel Island, southern Beaufort Sea, Yukon Territory, Canada. Geomorphology 95:84-102.

Lantz T. C., and S. V. Kokelj. 2008. Increasing rates of retrogressive thaw slump activity in the Mackenzie Delta region, N.W.T. Canada. Geophysical Research Letters 35: L06502.

Lawler, J. P., S. D. Miller, D. M. Sanzone, J. Ver Hoef, and S. B. Young. 2009. Arctic network vital signs monitoring plan. Natural Resource Report NPS/ARCN/NRR-2009/088. U.S.

Department of the Interior, National Park Service, Natural Resource Stewardship and Science, Ft. Collins, Colorado.

Lewkowicz, A. G. 2007. Dynamics of active-layer detachments failures, Fosheim Peninsula, Ellesmere Island, Nunavut, Canada. Permafrost and Periglacial Processes 18:89-103.

Lewkowicz, A. G., and C. Harris. 2005. Frequency and magnitude of active-layer detachment failures in discontinuous and continuous permafrost, northern Canada. Permafrost and Periglacial Processes 16:115–130.

Mackay, J. R., and S. R. Dallimore. 1992. Massive ice of the Tuktoyaktuk area, western Arctic coast, Canada. Canadian Journal of Earth Sciences 29(6):1235-1249.

Murton, J. B., C. A. Whiteman, R. I. Waller, W. H. Pollard, I. D. Clarke, and S. R. Dallimore. 2005. Basal ice facies and supraglacial melt-out till of the Laurentide Ice Sheet, Tuktoyaktuk Coastlands, western Arctic Canada. Quaternary Science Reviews 24:681-708.

Osterkamp, T. E., and V. E. Romanovsky. 1999. Evidence for warming and thawing of discontinuous permafrost in Alaska. Permafrost and Periglacial Processes. 10:17-37.

Swanson, D. K. 2010. Mapping of erosion features related to thaw of permafrost in Bering Land Bridge National Preserve, Cape Krusenstern National Monument, and Kobuk Valley National Park. Natural Resource Data Series NPS/ARCN/NRDS—2010/122. National Park Service, Fort Collins, Colorado.

Swanson, D. K. 2012. Monitoring of Retrogressive Thaw Slumps in the Arctic Network, 2011: Three-dimensional modeling of landform change. Natural Resource Data Series NPS/ARCN/NRDS—2012/247. National Park Service, Fort Collins, Colorado.

Swanson, D. K., and K. Hill. 2010. Monitoring of retrogressive thaw slumps in the Arctic Network, 2010 baseline data: Three-dimensional modeling with small-format aerial photographs. Natural Resource Data Series NPS/ARCN/NRDS—2010/123. National Park Service, Fort Collins, Colorado

Tucker C. J., and P. J. Sellers. 1986. Satellite remote sensing of primary production. International Journal of Remote Sensing 7(11):1395–1416.

US Geological Survey [USGS]. 2006. National elevation dataset. http://ned.usgs.gov/. Accessed 13 April 2010.

Western Regional Climate Center (WRCC). 2011. RAWS USA climate archives. http://www.raws.dri.edu/wraws/akF.html (accessed 12 April 2011).